In this book I have focused on the face adding supporting elements and innovative ways to use it expressively. These artistic projects are presented for you to duplicate or take the concepts and expand them with your own creativity. Some material substitutions may be necessary, but these are invitations to discover new possibilities. It is the process that is most important, particularly with face cane projects which can rarely be duplicated. You can apply these instructions to whatever face you like.

All of the projects are made with Prēmo polymer clay, a premium grade clay with colors designed for mixing. Polymer clay is an expressive medium that molds, carves, transfers and canes well. All clay techniques require practice, but they are possible for anyone to achieve.

In general, this book is designed for the craftsman already familiar with the product. Polymer clay is PVC and must be conditioned before use. This is usually done with a pasta machine and it is recommended that you be familiar with the machine and polymer clay tools. It is cured to a permanent and durable state by baking at 275° for 25 minutes. This information can easily be found in Design Originals Images on Clay I and II.

"How-to" photographs fill this book and make learning simple. Some steps are obvious, but still presented so you can see how things are done. Learn techniques by looking at the pictures and refer to valuable information that is explained in step-by-step directions.

Each project presents a challenge and a joyful experience. Once you are on the path, creative energy can hardly be contained. It gains momentum. You will become more skilled and inventive with practice. Every idea that sparks your imagination is a priceless gift that grows into a smile.

This book is dedicated to Norman Robinson (my friend with an encouraging smile).

Barbara A. McGuire

Wash your hands before and after using any clay. Keep your work surfaces clean. All of the clay must be conditioned before use.

Use a Pasta Machine for conditioning and sheeting clay. Knead or make clay pliable by running thin slices several times through the machine.

Clean machine between colors by running a paper towel through it several times.

Some ~~~~ than ot.

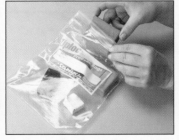

inclusions and the basic nature of the clay.

Blend clays to create any colors you will need.

Store new clay in heavy plastic freezer bags and air-tight containers away from heat and light.

Bake Clay according to manufacturers instructions.

I like to bake it on cardstock paper on a cookie sheet.

Using Images

The best advice is to use an image that you have permission to use.

Public Domain images, which include work published in the US before 1923, are generally available for use. Be aware that the copyright owner of a photograph may hold an additional copyright (Getting Permission by Stim Nolo Press).

may also use images mission, such as the ee images from most blications.

Rubber stamps from 'Angel companies' allow their stamps to be used in pieces created for sale.

These general rules should be researched according to your needs.

Many images are available through Web sites that offer clip art.

Fine art public domain images can be found at Corbis www.corbisview.com and archived photographs are at www.history.com.

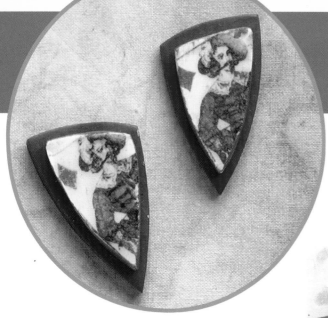

Unique Jewelry

Brighten up what's already in your closet with image transfer earrings. Transfer an image to clay, add a colorful clay backing and earring backs. The copper clay and gold leaf tile bracelet shows image transfers in the playing card design. The finished bracelet is sleek, smooth and unique!

  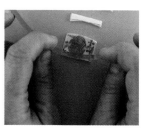

1 - 3 Place images on sheet of White clay 1/16" thick. Rub copy face down on clay to eliminate air pockets, mist with water. Saturate paper, do not use excessive amounts of water. Rub paper with your finger to shred paper from clay leaving the image. The image can be handled for approximately 1 hour. Place template over image 'cropping' the image as desired. Cut pairs for earrings. Flip template if using an asymmetrical shape. Trim or straighten shapes as needed by bending the blade and bearing down on edges.

4 - 6 Coat sides of earrings with rub-on metallics. Stack earring shape on 1/32" thick sheet of background clay. Bend blade and place just outside edge of the earring shape, cutting, leaving a slight border of color. Coat earring with Liquid Sculpey. Bake as manufacturer directs. Glue on earring backs.

Image Transfer Earrings
by Barbara A. McGuire

MATERIALS: *Premo* clay (White and background colors such as Copper. Gold or Black) • *Shapelets* earrings template • Mini metallic paint pots • Photocopy color transfer (see instructions for bracelet) • Post earring and earring nuts • *Liquid Sculpey* and application brush • Craft knife • Polymer blade • Super glue or 2-part Epoxy Glue • Water and misting bottle

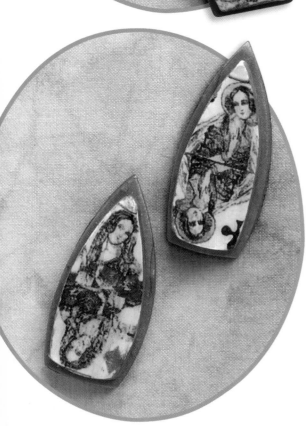

EARRING SHAPES
Cut 2 of each shape for each pair of earrings.

 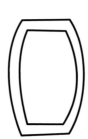 

Drill Hole

BRACELET TILE SHAPE

Drill Hole

BRACELET TILE SIDE VIEW

Hole

Back of Tile

Hole

Note how top and bottom edges of fronts of tiles are rounded.

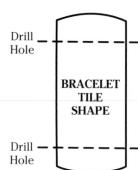

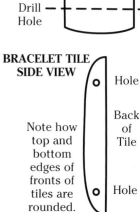

Expressions

Gold Leaf Tile Bracelet
by Barbara A. McGuire

MATERIALS: *Premo* clay (Copper, translucent) • Gold Leaf • *Liquid Sculpey* • Roller or pasta machine • Clay blade • Bone folder • Acrylic brayer • Transfer images or old playing cards • Water • Bowl • Drop of detergent • Soft cloth • Marking pen • Drill (*Dremel* hand or drill tool) • 400 and 600 Grit wet sandpaper • Buffing wheel (*Foredom* Jeweler's lathe muslin buffing wheels) • Stretch cord • Super glue • Purchase transfer images or photocopy provided images (Color copier that uses toner, not digital) on heavy coated paper (recommend *Hammermill* 28 pound color copier paper) • Images by *Bearing Beads*

INSTRUCTIONS: Condition clay, prepare a flat strip of Copper clay 1/4" thick x 2" x 8". Prepare a 2" x 8" strip of translucent clay very thin (#6 setting on Atlas pasta machine). Follow steps 1 - 12.

ASSEMBLY: Beginning at wide holes, thread tiles with stretch cord. Stuff ends in wide holes and dab with super glue.

1 - 5 Place images face down on translucent clay. Press to clay with bone folder to eliminate air pockets. Mist back of paper with water. When paper is wet, not dripping, shred paper away from clay, leaving the toner on clay. The toner will stay in place and image will be touchable. Place Gold leaf on Copper strip, spread and smooth with brayer. Leaf will crack slightly. Place a small amount of Liquid Sculpey on your finger, dab onto Gold leaf. This helps to adhere the translucent clay with the images.

6 - 8 Place the image strip on Gold leaf strip. The image should be next to the leaf and the translucent is on top. Smooth the layers with the brayer. Trim edges. Cut the bracelet into 1" wide sections. Smooth and taper edges of each tile before baking. Bake as manufacturer suggests.

9 - 12 After cooling, mark holes by marking in pairs. Holes will run horizontally through each tile at top and bottom. This will keep tiles from turning. Drill holes. Make one set of holes big enough to hide cord ends. Sand tiles with 400 and 600 grit wet sandpaper, adding water as you sand. A drop of liquid detergent in the water will help grit slide off the clay. Keep rinsing pieces clean, do not allow grit to dry. Buff on Foredom Buffing wheel at buffing speed (high). Use dust mask and safety precautions.

Photo Transfer

The paintings you see on this doll are from a series of work I painted several years ago. Now they will experience a new life as the expression on my doll. I tried several sizes before finding the right proportions to turn a painted face into a doll head.

These dolls make wonderful gifts. Design a collection and mount them on the wall.

Colorful Decorated Dolls Make Perfect Gifts!

1 - 3 Transfer photo to a sheet of White clay. Place the copy face down on clay, burnish it and mist with water until the paper is saturated. Shred the paper from clay until it reveals the copy. Trim the picture to an approximate size of the doll head. Place another image, prepared in the same fashion, on back side of doll head.

4 - 5 Align head sheets and press together, trim both sides and neck. Cover fabric on the doll head with Crafter's Pick glue or Liquid Sculpey. Cover the faces with Liquid Sculpey to protect against wear.

Photodoll
by Barbara McGuire

MATERIALS: White *Premo* clay • *Wild Woman* Cotton cloth body doll • Color toner photocopy on clay coated paper (28 pound *Hammermill* color copier paper) • Water and spray mister • Bone folder for burnishing paper to clay • Liquid Sculpey • X-acto knife • *Crafter's Pick* Ultimate Tacky Glue

INSTRUCTIONS: Size painting and have it photocopied. Ask the copy store if it can print on clay coated paper. This paper is preferred as it helps the toner rest on top of the paper instead of sinking into the fibers. Follow steps 1 - 5. Cloth will not burn at low oven temperatures. Bake complete doll to cure the clay as the manufacturer suggests.

& Rubber Stamp Dolls

This is a variation of the Photodoll which has a different look. Both dolls are designed for future decoration with beads, fibers, etc. Just glue or sew on embellishments.

Kids love experimenting and trying new things. This is a great project to share with young people. Let them use their own photo or one of a friend. The Stamped Doll is especially easy for young crafters to try. A win-win situation!

Note: Baking requires adult supervision.

Stamped Doll Head
by Barbara A. McGuire

MATERIALS: See Photodoll and substitute photocopy with items below: Lavender *Premo* clay (mix 1/4 Pearl Blue, 2/4 Pearl Red and 1/4 Pearl • *Judikins* Stamp Cube • *Pearl Ex* powder • *Sakura* Black Micro permanent fine point pen

1 - 2 Prepare doll by covering head with glue. Prepare a sheet of Lavender clay, mist lightly. Press the stamp into the clay.

3 - 4 Size clay to doll head. Trim excess.

5 - 6 Rub texture with Pearl Ex powders. Bake as manufacturer directs for curing clay. Outline stamped lines as desired in Black permanent marker.

Dolls Are Easy and Fun to Make!

'Madonna' Book

Record your thoughts in this spiritually designed book cover.

The wonder of reduction allows you to apply your face cane to any size project. For this reason, I keep portions of the cane in different diameters.

Madonna Book

By Barbara A. McGuire

MATERIALS: Light Turquoise *Premo* Pearl clay (Green Pearl and Blue Pearl mixed) • Rubber stamps (*Bearing Beads* Madonna outline; *Postmodern Design* • Water mist bottle • Slice of reduced Face Cane backed with White clay • *Pearl Ex* powders and application brush • Bone folder • Little paper book by *Graeham Owens* • *Crafters Pick* Ultimate Tacky Glue • *Tsukineko* Brilliance Platinum Planet ink • Silver embossing powder • Heat gun

1 - 3 Roll a sheet of the Turquoise clay, mist with water, and stamp impression of Madonna into clay. Reduce the face cane to fit in head of Madonna, slice and place on thin backing of White clay. Cut out head area from stamped image, replace with face cane slice. Smooth edges with bone folder. Color with Pearl Ex powders. Bake as manufacturer directs.

4 - 5 Mask out the corner of book with plain paper. Ink stamp, align the corners of the stamp and book, press to imprint. Repeat in opposite corner. Dust with embossing powder. Heat set ink and embossing powder on book with heat gun. When clay piece is cool, attach to cover of book with glue.

 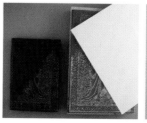 

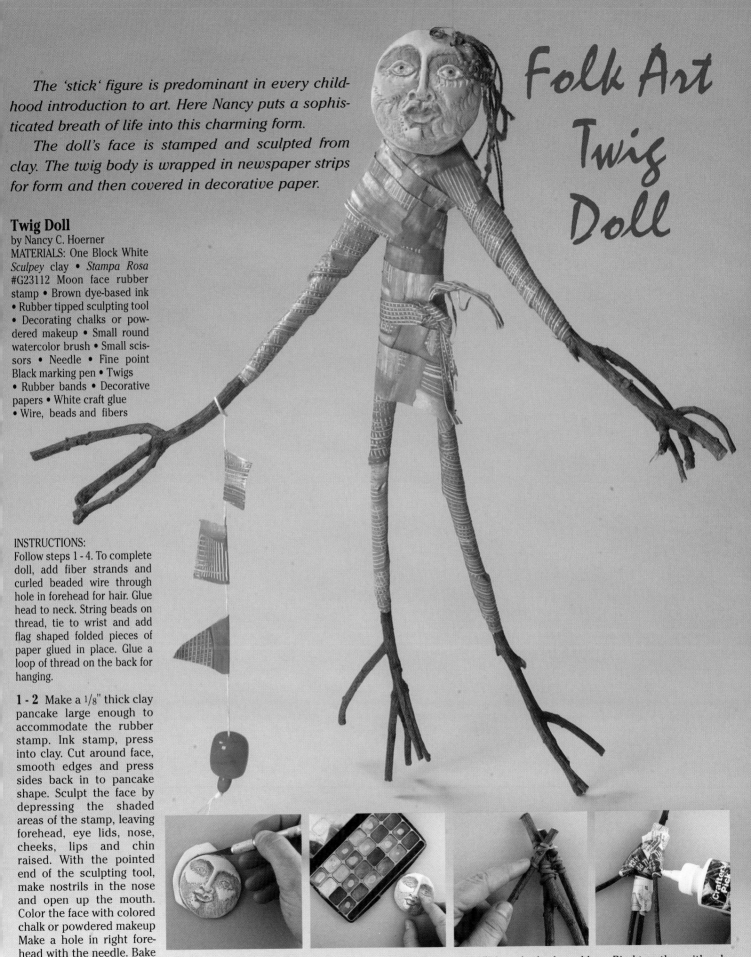

The 'stick' figure is predominant in every childhood introduction to art. Here Nancy puts a sophisticated breath of life into this charming form.

The doll's face is stamped and sculpted from clay. The twig body is wrapped in newspaper strips for form and then covered in decorative paper.

Folk Art Twig Doll

Twig Doll
by Nancy C. Hoerner

MATERIALS: One Block White *Sculpey* clay • *Stampa Rosa* #G23112 Moon face rubber stamp • Brown dye-based ink • Rubber tipped sculpting tool • Decorating chalks or powdered makeup • Small round watercolor brush • Small scissors • Needle • Fine point Black marking pen • Twigs • Rubber bands • Decorative papers • White craft glue • Wire, beads and fibers

INSTRUCTIONS:
Follow steps 1 - 4. To complete doll, add fiber strands and curled beaded wire through hole in forehead for hair. Glue head to neck. String beads on thread, tie to wrist and add flag shaped folded pieces of paper glued in place. Glue a loop of thread on the back for hanging.

1 - 2 Make a 1/8" thick clay pancake large enough to accommodate the rubber stamp. Ink stamp, press into clay. Cut around face, smooth edges and press sides back in to pancake shape. Sculpt the face by depressing the shaded areas of the stamp, leaving forehead, eye lids, nose, cheeks, lips and chin raised. With the pointed end of the sculpting tool, make nostrils in the nose and open up the mouth. Color the face with colored chalk or powdered makeup Make a hole in right forehead with the needle. Bake face as manufacturer directs. Color the pupils of the eyes with the Black marking pen.

3 - 4 Cut 2 twigs 10" long for arms. Cut 1 twig 14" and 1 twig 15" long for body and legs. Bind together with rubber band leaving one 1" above the other. Bind one arm at a time to the legs with a rubber band. Wrap body with 1" strips of newspaper to fill out the form. Glue as you wrap. Wrap arms and legs with decorative paper. Wrap body. Cut a strip of paper 1" x 12", fold in half, glue. Wrap the strip around waist, tie in place for the belt.

Fabulous Faces in Time...
Fashion Pins

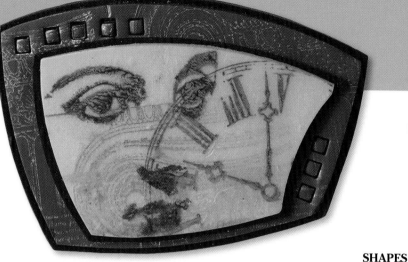

You can never have enough good pins.
Ones that puts real pizazz in your wardrobe.
These pins are a celebration of women, so
wear them proudly.

The clay is layered after being stamped
with   different colors. Dark color for focus
and a light color for filling the background.

Bent Frame Pins
by Barbara A. McGuire

MATERIALS: *Premo* Pearl clay in Black and Turquoise ($\frac{1}{2}$ Blue Pearl
and $\frac{1}{2}$ Green Pearl) • Inks(*Tsukineko* Brilliance Platinum;
Inkredible Gold Imprintz and Burnt Brass) • Flexible Super Slicer •
Limited Edition rubber stamps • Shapelet template • Nested square
punch cutter • Pin back • Craft knife • Super glue or 2-part epoxy

NOTE: If you are working on acrylic, your punched hole may not
lift; it is still cut but may adhere to the acrylic. If you are working
on card stock, punched hole should lift out.

INSTRUCTIONS: Condition and roll a flat sheet of light clay about
$\frac{1}{16}$" thick (#4 Atlas setting). This is your canvas. The stamps cho-
sen are for image, not depth, so they do not have to be deeply
etched. This formula for collage allows the colors and images to
balance. Follow instructions 1 - 13. Bake the piece at 275° for 20-25
minutes. Allow to cool. Piece may appear rubbery but will harden
as it cools. Add findings. Glue pin backs on with super glue or
epoxy. Optionally, re-bake after adding a thin layer of clay over bar
of pin back to hold it in place. Use Liquid Sculpey to attach baked
to unbaked clay, bake again as directed.

SHAPES
FOR PINS

Cut 1 Each
on
Solid Lines

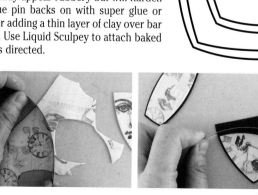
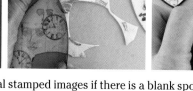

7 - 9 You can add additional stamped images if there is a blank spot in your
shape. Now make shapes of the remaining collage. Bend your blade randomly and create odd angles. You will get many pieces from one collage.
10 - 11 Leave an area large enough to punch little holes into it with cutter.

The punch works by pulling the inside back, pushing cutter into
clay, then pushing down to capture punched out piece.
12 - 13 Place artwork on another sheet of Black, bend blade, trim
very close to edge to frame and contrast shape. Add accent by

1 - 2 Stamp a face with a dark color for focus. Stamp a light color, Gold Imprintz with the column stamp over faces. This fills the background without competing with the face.

3 - 4 Use Burnt Brass from Inkredible to stamp clocks icon. Add a very light color with reflective quality, Tsukineko Platinum Planet, and use a 'writing stamp' over the whole piece. Do not touch ink once it is stamped. It will cure during baking. Clean your stamps with water or stamp cleaner.

5 Crop images with a clean Shapelet template. Lay template on clay to serve as a guide, cut clay with knife. Remove shape from body of the collage.

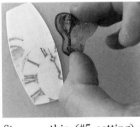

6 Place the cut shape on a very thin sheet of Black clay. Cut through the Black clay a slight distance from the edge of imaged shape. Bending the flexible clay blade to the curve of the shape will outline the shape, any width is fine.

Stamp a thin (#5 setting) sheet of Turquoise clay with script in Platinum Planet, repeating the writing in the collage. Place the edged shape on the stamped sheet, create interesting angles.

punching a smaller hole from scrap of turquoise sheet and inserting it into the larger holes from step 11. Carefully edge borders with metallic pigment. This helps to smooth edges.

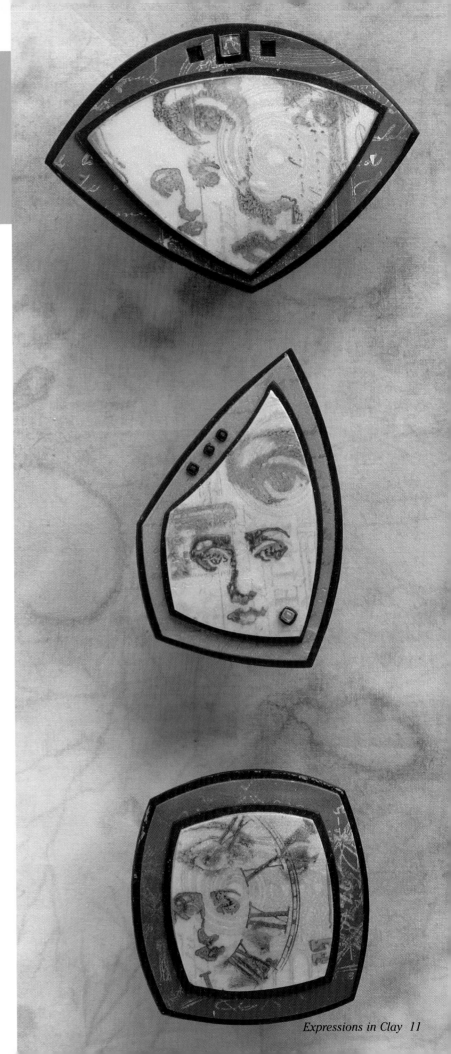

Metal Cloth Book
by Barbara A. McGuire

MATERIALS: *Premo* Pearl clay • *Inkredible ink* (Patina Beauty and Purple Eggplant) • *Postmodern Design* rubber stamp • Screw punch • Bone Folder • Eyelet & tabs • Eyelet setter & hammer • *Art–Forward* Metal cloth • Heavy pound watercolor cards • *Artistic* wire 20 gauge non-tarnish Silver • Two ⅛" brass tubes measured to fit the spine and one small tube to fit the clasp with ends filed smooth • Super glue • 1" Magnetic strip

NOTE: The original panels, cut to complement the size of the stamp, serve as a guide to determine the size of the book cover, which determined the size of the inside pages. There is no pattern as such.

I never can resist the urge to try new materials. The only aspect of this project I was familiar with was a simple stamped panel of polymer clay and that's enough for a great beginning.

The tools, eyelets, papers and brass rods, not to mention the magnet strips, all came together to give me confidence in making more creative and unique books.

1 - 5 Ink the stamp randomly with both colors, press image onto thin (#5 Atlas) sheet of Pearl polymer clay. Make 2 as front and back panels. Trim sheets. Bake as manufacturer directs. Lay panels on metal cloth, trim to book size. Lay another strip of metal cloth measured to wrap around the folded book, leaving ends extended 2". Fold book in half, score with bone folder. Middle band must be longer when book is folded. Place panel, punch a hole in each corner. Make hole slightly larger than eyelet. Slip eyelet in the hole from front to back, set the eyelets. Repeat with back panel. Inside of book has 3 metal cloth sheets nested into 3 cards. Cards were longer than the metal cloth and book covers so were bent back over the metal cloth to fit inside cover. Bend book in half to see how pages grow outward when nested. Crease edges.

6 - 10 When all the pages are in place, punch two holes in the spine of the book near the top and bottom. Cut 2 brass tubes, with filed ends, to fit between holes. Make inside hole short enough to slide back and over wire knot. Position tubes to be the backbone of spine, one on inside, one running along outside fold of cover. Thread wire through pages. Thread wire through the tubes on inside. Continue threading on outside. Join wires on inside of book. Slide tube to top, wrap wires together, cut and slide tube over wires to conceal. Glue magnets onto extended front band for magnet clasp. Center a tiny length of brass over edge of magnet to decorate the clasp.

Stamped Clay Charms

Beautiful Charms in No Time at All!

1 - 2 Ink stamp by laying rubber flat and tapping with ink pad. Stamp several images on thin sheet of White clay. Stamp another color on house stamps, inking only side portions of the stamp. Center over original stamped designs.

MATERIALS: *Premo* Polymer Clay (White; Translucent; Gold and Black to make Bronze) • *Zettiology* rubber stamps • *Inkredible* heat set inks (Midnight Blue, Purple Eggplant, Regal Burgundy) • Bone folder • Polymer clay blade • Roller • Needle tool • Wire rod to suspend beads while baking • *Kemper* graduated circle spring punch tools • Wire tools (flush cutters, round-nose and chain-nose pliers • 14 gauge Sterling wire • Cord or chain for hanging • Cardstock for baking surface • Small Silver beads with large holes for finishing

Stamped images courtesy of Zettiology

3 - 5 Cover stamped images with a very thin sheet of translucent clay, #7 setting on pasta machine, or as thin as possible, to imbed transfer so it can be touched. Trim the pieces. Wrap the bead with a cut square of images. Do not overlap image. Cut and trim where seams meet. Smooth seams together with the bone folder.

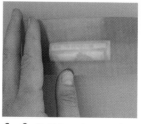 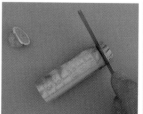 

6 - 8 Roll bead smooth on a firm surface, trim ends bearing down with the clay blade as you roll. Roll bead under an acrylic sheet to smooth and shape. Trim the ends if necessary. Prepare several sheets of clay to make end caps. They can be of varying thicknesses and colors. Punch out different diameters, center at each end of bead. Place small Silver ring beads at end. Poke a rod through the 2 ends and suspend bead during baking. Bake as directed. Alternately, use 16 or 18 gauge sterling wire to make a bail for the bead. Wire tools will be needed. Cut a 6" length and spiral one end leaving 4" free. Thread through bottom of bead. Turn a loop at top to make a loop.

Create charms that make great necklaces or will look terrific on your key chain too.

It's easy! Stamp clay images and roll clay into a bead. Trim out with different color end caps, silver or gold ring beads and finish with wire.

Elegant Beads, Keyrings and Charms!

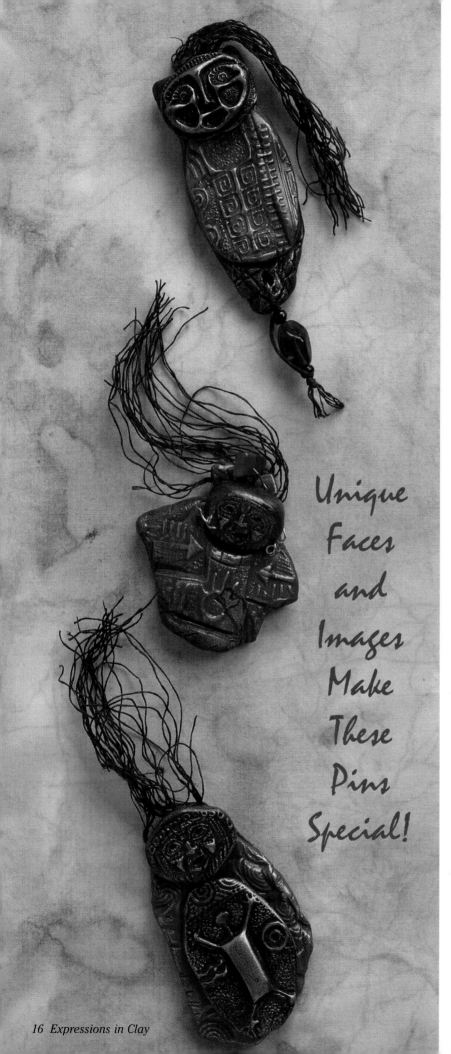

Primitive Stamped Art Pins

The theme of old world and primitive art images will always represent our connection to our past and gives us inspiration for the future. The stamped faces and images of ancient spirits give these pins a mystical appearance resembling unique, old world primitive art objects. These stamps, created by Sherrill Kahn, inspire us to use creativity to display our individuality, spirit, love and willingness to connect with each other.

Unique Faces and Images Make These Pins Special!

Stamped images
courtesy of
Impress Me

Old World Primitive Art Pins

by Diane Flowers

NOTE: Individual pieces may not use all materials listed.
MATERIALS: *Premo* clay (Black, Raw Sienna, Copper, Gold) • *Impress Me* unmounted rubber stamp sets • Black waxed linen string • Gold metallic rub-on • *Pearl Ex* powders • Matte finish varnish • Super glue • Pin back • Shaping tool • Needle tool • Accent beads • 24 gauge Gold wire
INSTRUCTIONS: Follow steps 1 - 6. Bake face and body shapes according to manufacturer's directions. Follow steps 7 - 8. Super glue head to body. Glue on pin back, varnish entire piece to protect finish. For additional interest and variation, adorn with accent beads, Gold wires and waxed linen cords.

Stamped images courtesy of Impress Me

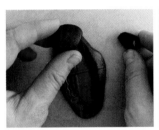

1 - 2 Condition and mix slightly blended clay colors into an interesting shape, approximately 1/8" thick for body. Lightly mist clay with water as a release, press stamp into body. Use stamps pressed in different directions to add interest and create design groupings. Make 3 large holes approximately 1/8" from top of body shape large enough for waxed linen strand or strands. Bottom hole is optional.

3 - 4 Make a smaller shape of solid black clay until the size is appropriate for the head. Mist and press into rubber stamp over face.

5 - 6 Highlight raised surfaces with metallic rub-ons. Add color with Pearl Ex powders.

7 - 8 When piece is cool, thread the linen cord or cords through the hole and double knot. Separate the threads to create 'hair' or cut multiple cords into varying lengths.

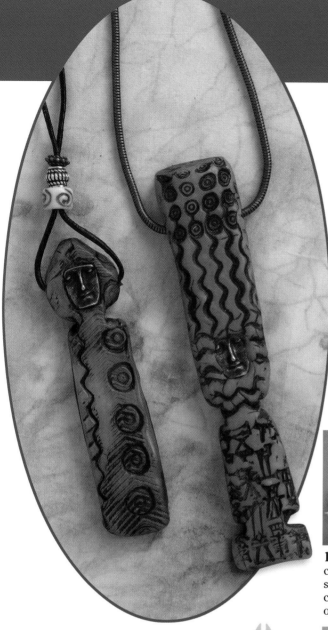

Polymer clay molds can be made from almost anything. Mold faces from sources such as buttons, carvings, dolls, statues and originals you have fashioned yourself. The intention of molding here is to create something new or to alter and duplicate an interpretation of your own. It is unethical to make a mold for the purpose of duplicating and selling exactly what the original artist or manufacturer is selling.

It is unethical to sell a mold of what another artist or manufacturer has created. Do not mold an item with copyright markings.

It is fun and challenging to create a new piece of art or to use pieces to make an individual whole.

1 - 3 Mix color by spreading extremely thin sheets of colored clay over translucent clay. Do not over-blend, solid color will result. Layer clay into sheets, stack until slab is 1/4" thick. Place template on slab, trim around template to cut shape. Place cut shape on rubber texture sheet, press additional textures onto top of shape.

Dream Doll Pendant
by Barbara A. McGuire

MATERIALS: Mixed *Premo* clay (1 block Translucent, dime size ball of Gold, pea size ball of Green) • *Art-Forward* Doll template or create a shape from paper • Purchased bead face or carved bone face • *Art- Forward* rubber texture sheets, geometric and language designs • Misting bottle • Polymer Blade • Craft knife • Bone burnisher • Drill • *Golden* Raw Umber acrylic paint • Application brush • Soft cloth

INSTRUCTIONS: Follow steps 1 - 6. Bake as manufacturer directs. Poke a hole through the pendant for cord before baking or drill the hole after baking. Cool. Follow steps 7 - 9. If drilling hole, use dremel hand drill or double-ended drill tool horizontally through upper portion of pendant. Hole must be large enough to fit cords. Lace cord through, add beads if desired.

4 - 6 The shape will become distorted with pressure, use side of polymer blade to push and straighten back into shape. Use a bone folder to indent the smaller corners of the shape. Cut a hole, insert face bead. The bead used is double-sided and very thick. If using a shallow bead, see instructions on inserting molded faces.

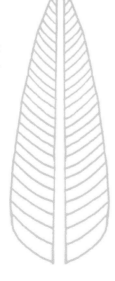

Stamped images courtesy of Art-Forward by Barbara McGuire.

7 - 9 Trim excess clay from around face bead. Brush on acrylic paint. Wipe raised surface with damp cloth to remove excess. Paint will set in 24 hours.

Textured Primitive Pendants

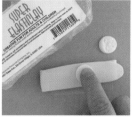   

1 - 4 Condition Elasticlay, create a smooth slab deep enough to accommodate what you are molding. Dust with cornstarch. Press item into slab. For odd sizes or doll impressions, push clay up around object if needed to fill any gaps left by pushing on clay. Bake mold. Roll smooth ball of clay and push into mold. Form excess into a handle shape.

5 - 6 Pull molded piece from mold. Cut excess with blade, rotating as you cut.

7 - 8 Stretch or push the molded face as desired to create new interpretations of the original. Bake molded face. Press outline of baked face into clay doll, remove and carve out the space with a wire clay tool.

9 - 10 Smooth the space with Liquid Sculpey to assure there are no air bubbles. Adhere baked face into unbaked pendant. Bake piece as manufacturer suggests.

Molded Faces

MATERIALS: Objects to mold
• *Sculpey* Super Elasticlay
• Mister bottle • Cornstarch
GENERAL INSTRUCTIONS: Follow steps 1 - 4. If mold, metal, bone, etc., can tolerate oven temperatures, bake clay object in the mold. If it is a resin, remove from mold before baking. Bake as manufacturer suggests. When cool, pop out molded piece.
TIP: Molds can also be made from regular polymer clay but will not be flexible.

To Make A Duplicate From A Mold

MATERIALS: Clay • Mold
• Mister bottle of water
INSTRUCTIONS: Follow steps 1 - 7. Bake according to manufacturer's directions. To prepare a doll pendant as described in the Dream Doll project, follow steps 8 - 10.

Masks in Clay with Wire & Ribbon

In creating this delightful Jester, Alba Monros lent me the face and mold she had made from Sculpey Terra Cotta.

The original mold had a garden clay look and feel. I want-ed to duplicate them to keep as refined as possible. The sec-ond generation of results were as lovely as the first.

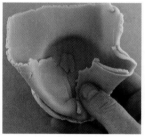 

1 - 2 Dust original face with cornstarch to act as a release. Make a mold of original face with Super Elasticlay. Push clay up around the face. Pull the mold from the original and bake as manufacturer directs. Prepare a flat sheet of Beige clay. Dust mold with corn-starch, press sheet into mold.

Jester Mask on a Stand

MATERIALS: *Sculpey* Super Elasticlay • Beige *Premo* • Sculpted clay face • Cornstarch • Fluffy brush • Dowel • *Artistic* Wire • Gold leaf •Flush cutters, round-nose pliers and chain-nose pliers • Ribbons and fibers • Optional: *Golden* Iridescent Gold acrylic paint

3 - 7 Fold edges into the center to fill back of head. Carefully remove head from mold. Make 2. Place the 2 heads together over dowel. Smooth seam carefully, handling the faces lightly putting pressure on the edges. Place on bed of fiberfill to support head while you work. You will also bake on this material to keep features of face. Form a big dome, cover with Gold leaf. Some leaf has patterns already in it. Stick the dowel into dome base to make a hole. Set aside to bake.

8 - 12 Using round-nose pliers, turn end of wire into a spiral. Using chain-nose pliers to hold spiral horizontally, continue to wind wire around itself, pushing with your thumb. Cut the wire when spiral is length you want. Make 20 spirals from different colors. Stick spirals into seam of jester head. Bake (on fiberfill) as manufacturer directs. After baking, dust cornstarch on one side of a sheet of colored clay, lay over the face,dust side down and sketch out a mask. Cut to shape and bake again over face using face for its form. Mask can also be covered with Gold leaf. Paint face Iridescent Gold. To finish jester, weave ribbons through wires, knot together at each side of face. Let ribbons dangle. Drill holes in mask, tie to wire. Paint or cover dowel with ribbon. Glue dowel into dome holder. Spiral ribbons around neck of dowel for decorative collar.

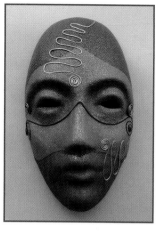

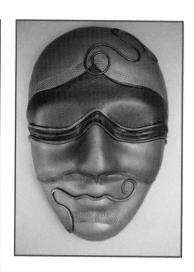

Wall Masks "Expressions"

Attention mask lovers! Make your own masks!

The mask here was created by laying clay colors over a base mask and then adding sections of chain for trim. Simple lines are easy and elegant.

Clay Covered Mask

by Barbara A. McGuire

MATERIALS: *Premo* metallic and pearl clay • Base mask that can stand oven temperatures of 265° • Sections of chain • Flush cutters • Craft knife • Flush cutters • Crafter's Pick Ultimate Tacky Glue Super glue to secure chain • Permanent marker pen

INSTRUCTIONS: Follow steps 1-10. Bake mask at 265° for 20 minutes or as manufacturer suggest After it cools, drill a hole in the side and attach decorative cords or wire to the mask for hanging. Cu holes in eyes if you want to wear the mask. If the chain is not securely embedded into the clay, it ca be super glued in place after baking.

1 - 5 All sheets should be same thickness. Prepare sheets of clay as follows: 1/8 Green pearl with 1 block Gold, 1/2 Red pearl with 1/2 Blue pearl 1/2 Green pearl with 1/2 Blue pearl, 1/4 Purple (Red & Blue) with 1 block pearl. Draw on mask dividing mask into sections defining the lines tha accentuate the curves of the face. Coat mask with glue, let dry. Cover mask with clay, arranging colors as you choose. Use a craft knife to cu edge of lines. Overlap each layer, do not press together. Clay will create a line as a guide for you to cut.

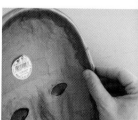

6 - 10 Smooth the seams with your fingers. When mask is covered, place chain on the piece. After chain pieces are arranged, press gently bu securely into the mask. Clip ends of chain with flush edge of cutters. Add any additional trim. Smooth edges.

Beautifully

Alba's Lady of the Woods

by Alba Monros

MATERIALS: *Super ELasticlay* • *Premo* Pearl, Red pearl, Blue pearl, Green Pearl and Translucent • *Liquid Sculpey* • Carved face or doll face • *Art–Forward* Garden Texture sheet • *Graeham Owens* Paper book • Cardstock • *Tsukineko* Platinum Planet ink • *Pearl Ex* powders • *Loew Cornell* soft application brush • Decorating chalks • *Cool Tool* • Super Slicer Blade • *Crafter's Pick* Ultimate Tacky Glue

1 Dust the original face with cornstarch to act as a release. Make a mold of original face with Super Elasticlay. Push clay up around the face. Pull the mold from the original, bake according to manufacturer's directions.

2 - 6 Condition translucent clay, form into a shape that will fit mold. Nose should be extended ready to push into deepest place in mold. Mist with water to act as a release. Push firmly into mold. Release shaped face from mold. Correct profile if needed with Cool Tool. Mix decorating chalks with Liquid Sculpey, paint lips and eyes. Very lightly dust cheeks with chalk. Color headdress with Pearl Ex using soft brush.

 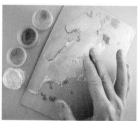 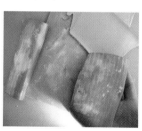  

7 - 11 Slice off any excess to even doll head. Back can still be hollow. Size sheet of pastel clay to fit book cover, rub with different colors of Pearl Ex powder. Use excess of powders to tint sheets of clay for gown and cape. Press texture stamps into cover panel to create imprinted designs. Trim edges, tap with blade to make even and smooth.

12 - 16 Stamp book cover with ink using one leaf design from texture sheet. Cut out individual stamped leaves, smooth the sides. Place leaves on book to nest head. Use Liquid Sculpey to assure adhesion through powdered clay. Place head on bed of leaves. Make a sausage body of scrap clay. Cover with draped pastel layers to suggest a gown and cape. Add ribbon of clay to create a scarf, hide edges. Bake following manufacturer's instructions. Glue to book when cool.

Molded & Draped Lady

Alba's 'Lady' was so beautiful that I wanted to duplicate it asclosely as possible. The results were a likeness with subtle variations. Draping' sheets of clay was the biggest challenge of the project.

Conceptual Doll Art

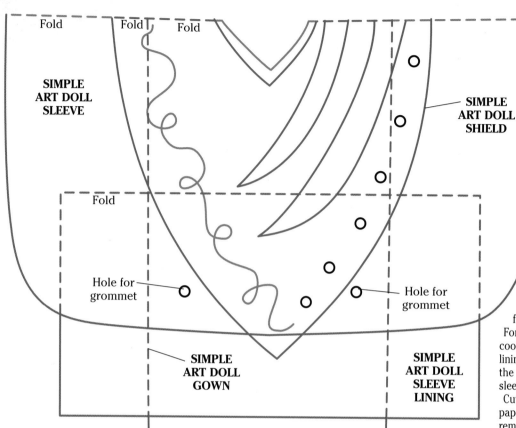

Fold   Fold   Fold

**SIMPLE
ART DOLL
SLEEVE**

**SIMPLE
ART DOLL
SHIELD**

Fold

Hole for
grommet

Hole for
grommet

**SIMPLE
ART DOLL
GOWN**

**SIMPLE
ART DOLL
SLEEVE
LINING**

**DOLL
NECKLACE**

Thread
beads as
shown, pull
taut. Thread
cord through
grommet
holes and tie
off at charm.
Trim cord.

Sometimes you can capture the essence, aura and concept of a work in a moment. When I first looked at Judith's doll, I wanted to immediately replicate it with my own inspiration. This is already a second generation doll since Judith was instructed by Barbara Miller of Amadore, Pennsylvania. It is always fitting to acknowledge the artist who has influenced your creations. No matter how much things are changed, the life of the idea remains to generate new interpretations and delight future artists. Thank you to all the persons who have contributed to the heart of this doll.

Ulysses-San Art Doll

by Judith T. Oruska

MATERIALS: 4 Coordinated papers o fabrics • Small piece of clay • *Pape Parachute* Moon Face rubber stamp • Narrow cords, beads, charms, ril bons, glitter and embellishments • 1/8" Grommets and setter • Dent floss • Drill • Plaque or block of woo for base • Fine to medium sandpape • 2 Pair chopsticks or dowels jus over 10" long • E-6000 Glue

INSTRUCTIONS:

For the body, select 2 pair of qualit chopsticks, or use dowels. Separat and trim one pair to be 7 1/2" long. Tri the other pair to a little more than 10 Sand rough edges to resemble chopstic ends. Lash the 2 sets together with dent floss to form body, arms and legs.

For the costume, select 4 types of paper that ar coordinated or fabrics for gown, sleeves, sleev lining and shield. Cut front and back of gown o the fold. Cut an oblong shape on the fold fo sleeves. Round the corners.

Cut the shield on the fold from a 3rd selecte paper. Cut slashes on one side of shield. Us remaining papers as sleeve lining. Cut one na row rectangle from this paper. Round the co ners. If this paper is very thin, cut 2 sheets, glue togethe. Cut a V slit in the neck of gown, sleeve and shield pieces Decorate gown, sleeves and shield with ribbons, glitte and embellishments.

Assemble the doll by nesting gown, sleeve and shield over the head of the leg-arm assembly. Glue fro and back together. Poke 1/8" grommets through costum at waist, tie narrow cording around figure. Add bead and charms to dangle from ties.

Press a face stamp, *Paper Parachute's* Moon face o other, into a piece of clay. Trim, leaving shape of mask Poke a hole through sides for hanging. Use a ball of ti foil to support the shape, bake as manufacturer directs Mask can be painted after baking, if desired. Pass Gol thread through holes, tie knots and fringe the ends Sanded scrap lumber or a wooden plaque from a craf store can be used for the base.

Paint base Gold. Drill 2 holes slightly larger than th legs, insert legs into holes. Wrap the mask around th neck. Select a suitable haiku, print it onto parchment P22's Da Vinci font is a good choice.

Trim edges with decorative scissors and Gold ink Wrap top of parchment around a bamboo stick, glue t itself. Roll bottom of parchment around a knitting nee dle. When released, it should coil.

Glue to base.

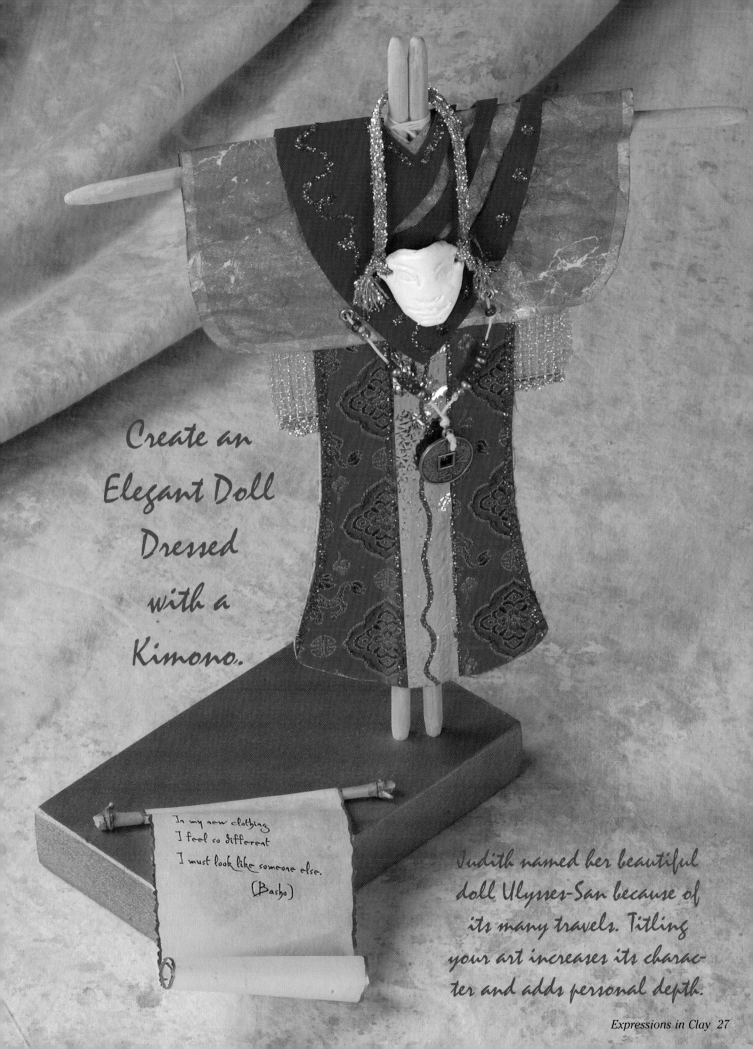

Create an
Elegant Doll
Dressed
with a
Kimono.

In my new clothing
I feel so different
I must look like someone else.
(Basho)

Judith named her beautiful
doll Ulysses-San because of
its many travels. Titling
your art increases its charac-
ter and adds personal depth.

Romney - Woodland Sprite

This is Romney, a young sprite who is just beginning to discover what life is all about. Rebecca has created a charming world in her projects.

Inspired by artists who have discovered other worlds within the realms of creativity, you are invited to explore your own imaginary concepts.

   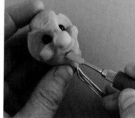

1 - 4 Condition clay, roll into ball about the size of a walnut, roll into an egg shape. Pinch sides to create ears and area between to create the bridge of nose and upper lip. Roll a pea size ball, cut in half and place each in cheek area on either side of nose. With a round rolling tool such as a crochet hook handle, roll cheeks into face, blending together. First roll cheek towards eyes, then out into ears, forward into bridge of nose and down toward mouth. Be careful only to roll edges of cheek ball, not the whole thing. Place indentions in ears and round spots where eyes will be placed. Put beads in place pushing into eye sockets deep enough that bead hole just barely sinks into cavity. For placing beads, a darning needle works well. Position bead hole so that one opening points to bridge of nose and one points toward ear. Place another round ball of clay onto nose, roll into face starting at top, then underneath into lip area, being careful not to roll upper lip away. Roll out sides toward cheek. Start shaping upper lip, define smile or shape of mouth.

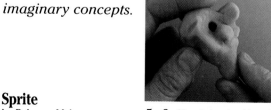 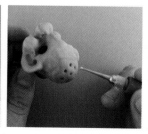 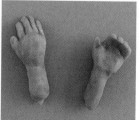 

Sprite
by Rebecca Malone
MATERIALS: *Super Sculpey*
• 5mm Black glass beads
• Crochet needle • Pencil
• Armature wire • Cloth strip
for clothes

5 - 8 Check back of head. Add more clay if necessary to fill it out and give a realistic shape. Add a pea size ball of clay to create chin. Blend in without damaging other features. Inset wires into head far enough to insure a sturdy neck. Doubling the wires into hairpin shapes provides more surface for clay to adhere to. Shape neck and throat bringing down clay from back of head, under chin and ear area. Make nostrils with a sharp tool. Continue to define mouth and lips. Shape ears, press a few wrinkles into forehead. Shape hands. Bake clay as manufacturer directs. Wrap cloth around sprite to create body. Attach hands. Dress as desired.

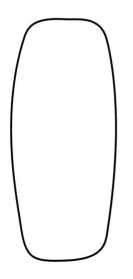

Cropped Pin

by Barbara A. McGuire

MATERIALS: *Premo* clay in Pearl, Bronze (Black and Gold mixed), Olive Green (Blue and Gold mixed) and Black • Japanese face cane • Super Slicer • Bone folder • Claystamp by Nan Roche, Chinese negative impression stamp • Water mister • Pasta machine fettuccini attachment • Pin-back • Super glue

PIN SHAPES

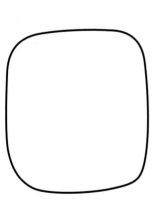

1 - 2 Create a Mokume Gane stack by layering thin Black, Green, Bronze and White sheets of clay. Stack and run through pasta machine. Divide, restack, run again through machine until you have 12 extremely thin striped layers.

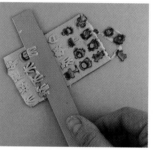

3 - 5 Mist clay stamp, press clay stack into stamp. Release. Clay will have a raised image. Slice off the characters that have raised up. Roll a sheet of Pearl clay. Position a slice of the face cane on the sheet.

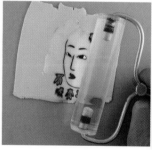

6 - 8 Shave edge of the face cane slice until it is flush with background clay. Graft portions of clay to cover pin area. Shave portions from back and top of face, place it on bottom and side to cover the entire area you want to use. Place the little shaved characters on the clay. Roll grafted art smooth with acrylic brayer.

9 - 11 Use a Shapelets template to crop face and characters. With craft blade cut out pin shape. Add layers of clay under original work to thicken the cut shape to ¼". Trim shape. Run a thin sheet (#5 Atlas) of Bronze clay through fettuccini attachment, producing thin strips. Cut a beveled edge on end of 1 strip, begin wrapping around sides of work, starting in lower corner. When wrap is complete, bevel opposite edge, smooth join with bone folder. Bake as directed. Attach pin back with super glue.

Cane Pins

It's hard to believe that these beautiful pins are made from clay. The ivory colored clay looks like real ivory inlayed with other exotic stones.

This look was achieved by creating a Mokume Gane stack first. Mixing clay colors with pearl white sheets of clay ultimately gives the clay a pearlized look.

See the following pages for more creative caning ideas! Remember, every idea that sparks your imagination is a priceless gift that grows into a smile.

The Joys of Clay Caning

On these pages I show how many different looks you can achieve through making canes. They are shown actual size so that you can see how much detail can be created through this process. To get started, follow the easy step photos below that show how to make a small flower cane.

Small Flower Cane for Embellishment

MATERIALS: *Premo* Clay (Metallic Purple, Lavender, Lime) • blade to cut clay • 1 yard Black leather cord

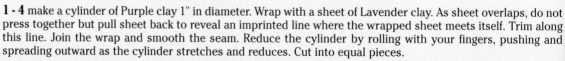

1 - 4 make a cylinder of Purple clay 1" in diameter. Wrap with a sheet of Lavender clay. As sheet overlaps, do not press together but pull sheet back to reveal an imprinted line where the wrapped sheet meets itself. Trim along this line. Join the wrap and smooth the seam. Reduce the cylinder by rolling with your fingers, pushing and spreading outward as the cylinder stretches and reduces. Cut into equal pieces.

7 - 11 Assemble flower by alternating petal and triangle. When you are halfway through, add a small snake of clay for the center. Spread Lime triangles over entire outside of cane, add more clay where needed. Roll smooth, reduce pieces of this cane to several different diameters, cutting into sections for future use. Cut small disks by rolling the cane and slicing across the design. These slices will decorate your work.

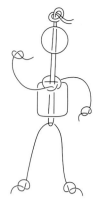

Cane Face and Bead Dolls

Assembly

Note: These dolls are a variation of the doll on page 37. Here I used applied cane slices on beads for the body.

by Barbara A. McGuire

General instructions for this type of doll are given on page 37. Create the beads by first making canes. Cut cords for necklace, arms and legs. Tie knots at ends of short cords for hands and feet. Thread both ends of long cord through bottom of body. In this case body is a bead. Do not pull completely through, keep loop at bottom of body bead. Thread both ends of long cord through bottom of head. The head will sit on top of body. Slip feet cord through loop and bottom of body, pull taut to secure. Pressure will keep feet cord in place and prevent neck cord from pulling through. Separate head from body, tie arms cord around neck. Pull or push everything into place, tie ends of long cord together.

5 - 6 Pinch cane on one end to make a teardrop. Make a 1½" barrel of Lime clay. Cut downward as if you are cutting pie sections to divide clay into 6 pieces. Pinch these section into triangles.

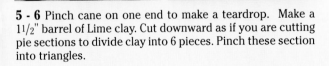

Cane slices will decorate your work!

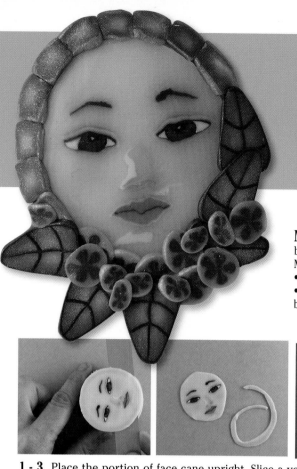

Cane Faces
with Embellishments

Mosaic Framed Face Pins
by Barbara A. McGuire
MATERIALS: White *Premo* clay • Slice of face cane
• Leaf cane • Flower cane • Simple shaded cane
• *Super Sculpey* slicer • *Excel* blade • Concho • Pin
back • Super glue

*This project
is a great way to
decorate with a variety of canes
from different projects. The face is
surrounded and supported by theme
designs. These groupings unify and
strengthen the composition. When
you become familiar with canes, you
will appreciate how long they last
and the different ways to use them.*

1 - 3 Place the portion of face cane upright. Slice a very thin layer horizontally across top. The thinner the layer, the more delicate the translucent face will seem. Trim cane slice to shape you want face to be. Place face slice on a sheet of White clay (#1 Atlas). This is so translucent clay is 'illuminated'.

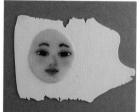

4 - 6 Reduce decorative canes to various sizes. Cut thin slices of leaf, flowers and shaded cane. Place on White clay sheet surrounding face. Group as desired, with symmetry or not, assembling small cane slices in repetitive orders. Cut out entire shape with Excel blade. Mold piece over concho to give it a slight curve and add depth to form. Bake as manufacturer directs. Cool, attach pin back with glue.

Graduated Blend Leaf Cane

1 - 5 Make a sheet of skinner blended colors. Place sheet in pasta machine at light end of blend. Stretch sheet to thinnest setting. Sheet will be very long. Roll it up, starting with lightest color. Work it back into a larger diameter by pushing and rolling inward. Cut leaf into sections to suggest veins. Insert a very thin sheet of Brown between sections, reassemble leaf. Wrap outside of leaf with a thin sheet of Brown.

Make leaf, flower and assorted canes.

Roll the canes into different diameters. This will provide you with designs of varying sizes that you can use to embellish faces.

These wonderful pins were created with an assortment of canes.

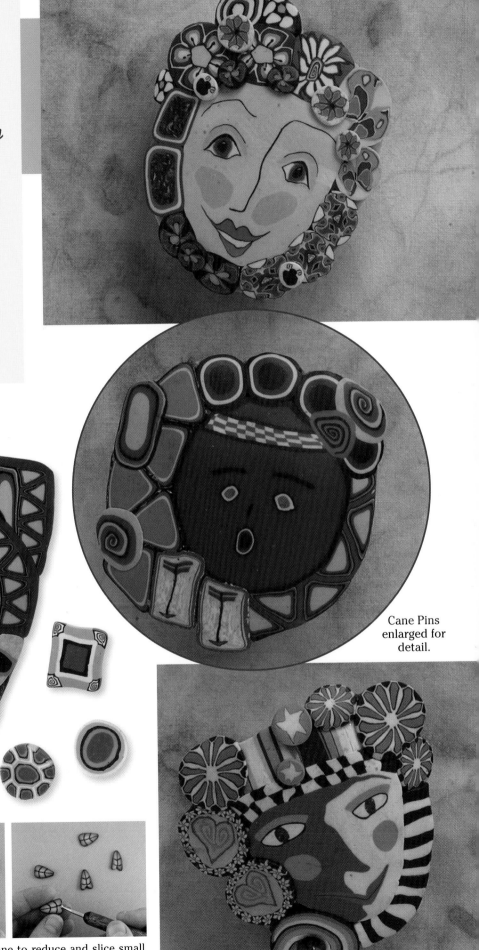

Cane Pins enlarged for detail.

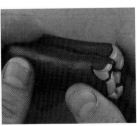
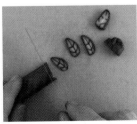

6 - 8 Press cane into a teardrop leaf shape. Pull cane to reduce and slice small leaves. Use small embossing tool to further shape leaf.

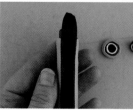

1 - 5 Mix Flesh color. Condition other colors. Beginning with eyes, roll tiny snake of Black, surround with layer of Violet. Trim wrapped clay to meet exactly, important for all wrapped layers. Roll thin sheet of White, wrap eye. Wrap with Black, then Flesh. Black layer should be very thin, to outline eye. Flesh layer surrounds entire eye and all face parts, eye, nose and mouth. Make strip of clay for brow, no wider than eye, taper on 1 side with roller, wrap with Flesh. Position on top of eye, wrap with Flesh.

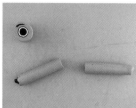

6 - 10 Trim to meet exactly, smooth join. Cut eye cane in half. Cut off ends to make sure design goes through entire cane. Keep slices for comparison and help with placement and proportion. Set aside. Make shapes that will define nose, 1 long strip with 2 side units for nostrils. Make the nose smaller than you think. Noses will grow. Wrap nose in very thin sheet of Black, make sure sheet fits exactly around the shape. Wrap with flesh.

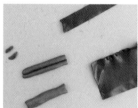

11 - 15 Check clay seam. Cut a piece off to see how outline is embedded and creates nose shape. Mouth is made of 1 half circle for bottom lip, 2 smaller half circles for top lip. Use thin sheets to wrap around mouth and a strip for smile line. Place strip of clay for smile line between top and bottom lips. Wrap entire lip in very thin sheet of Black. Center small triangle of Flesh on top lip to maintain wedge in top lip. Wrap lip with Flesh.

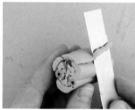

17 - 21 Make sure nose is directly on top of mouth for entire strip. Align back of face cane. Trim uneven lengths resulting from reduction. Place small triangular shapes in gaps in face. Add larger portions of clay to define forehead and cheeks. Condition, pack rectangular slab of Gold clay. Slice away clay on outside to define shape of face.

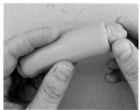

26 - 30 You can insert a plug at cane end to help keep outer layers from moving faster than inner layers. Eventually you will be able to roll the cane on a flat surface to even it out. Slice until the face shows. Reduce the face to size needed. Cut face cane in half to add different hair-dos. Condition a slab of Gold clay. Slice vertically with wavy blade. Place sheets of Black clay between cut Gold waves, reassemble Gold slab.

36 - Use wavy blade to trim stripes and create a permed look. Keep cane in small heavy plastic bag, or wrap with heavy plastic to store until needed. Slice face cane into 1/2" sections for as many dolls as needed. Make hole vertically through center of head, bake following manufacturer's directions. **37 - 42** Create body by placing sheets of clay over paper cone, join seams. Mist clay, stamp design into body. Trim cone.

Bead Buddies

Making a simple face is fun, easy and can be used in many applications. This doll was inspired by a young artist learning crafts on her 8th birthday. Throughout the years the doll took many forms, but never lost its original charm.

A simple standard method is used to make this face, a good beginning to understanding placement and proportions of features. Additional important points are to use very thin sheets to outline features and to always wrap features totally in flesh to smooth and secure the shapes.

Bead Buddy
by Barbara A. McGuire

MATERIALS: *Premo* clay (Ecru, Copper, Gold, Black, Red, White, Blue, Violet) • Face color clay (2 blocks Ecru to 1/8 block metallic Copper) • Clay shaping tools • Wavy cutting blade

Instructions for Buddy Body
MATERIALS: *Premo* metallic clay mixed colors (Olive - 1/2 Green Pearl and 1/2 Gold; Purple - 1/2 Red Pearl and 1/2 Blue Pearl • Face cane • Paper cone • *Kemper* punches • *Stamplets* heart rubber stamp • 1 Yard leather cord • Leather cords 6" and 8" long
INSTRUCTIONS: Follow steps 37 - 40.

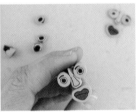

16 - Place eyes, nose and mouth together, compare size. Reduce any proportions that are too big.

22 - 25 Wrap entire face with sheet of Flesh. Slice end and face appears. Roll cane smooth in both directions, flip cane occasionally to prevent twisting as pressure applied is usually uneven.

31 - 35 Reduce cane, taper it on one end. This will be part in hair. Slice a portion, position on face cane. Use wavy blade again to cut waves along ends of hair. Use wavy blade to shape outside of hair. Make another hairdo by slicing surface of hair and adding stripes around outside of head.

Frill edges. Stamp and punch out small circles, place on body to decorate. Bake body as manufacturer directs. Cut cords for necklace, arms and legs. Tie knots at ends of short cords for hands and feet. Thread both ends of long cord through bottom of body. Do not pull completely through, keep loop at bottom of body bead. Thread both ends of long cord through bottom of head. The head will sit on top of body. Slip feet cord through loop and bottom of body, pull taut to secure. Pressure will keep feet cord in place and prevent neck cord from pulling through. Separate head from body, tie arms cord around neck. Pull or push everything into place, tie ends of long cord together.

Heritage Cards

Sally used pictures of her relatives on these special cards. Her talent in layering different papers and shapes was inspiration for the romantic card I constructed from her directions. Enjoy!

by Sally Evans
MATERIALS: Translucent *Liquid Sculpey (TLS)* • Photograph or image photocopied on a toner based copier onto color copier paper • Oven • Piece of glass or cardstock to bake on • Coordinating card, papers, vellum, etc. • Scissors, rulers, pencil • Eyelets and setting tools • *Shapelets* Heart template • *Excel* craft blade

1 - 2 I did a test to see which papers worked best. The glossy paper bubbled. The ultimate performance was achieved with a toner copier. I used a Canon personal copier, which produced a bluish transfer, copied onto Hammermill 28 pound color copier paper.

3 - 4 Cut out photocopied image with at least 1/2" margin around it. Pour or brush TLS on image. Use finger or brush to make a smooth even layer. Bake at 275° for 15 minutes in a well-ventilated room. Peel off paper while Liquid Sculpey is warm.

5 - 6 If there is any excess paper, soak transfer in water, rub paper off. Use Templates shapelet to cut postage heart out of transfer.

Knowing that individual copiers and papers can produce different results, I did a test to see which papers worked best. My glossy paper bubbled.

The best performance was achieved with a toner copier.

I used a Canon personal copier, which produced a beautiful bluish transfer, copied onto Hammermill 28 pound color copier paper.

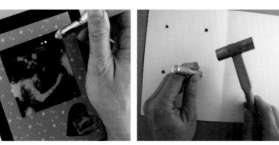

7 - 8 Trim and align images as desired. Use a screw punch to make eyelet holes in corners. Set eyelets from back of card cover.

Use These Techniques for Elegant Tools

Skinner Blend for Topped Tool and Adorned Tool

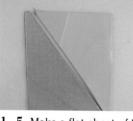 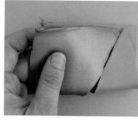 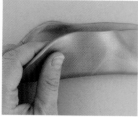  

1 - 5 Make a flat sheet of 2 long right triangles of colors to blend, turquoise and gold shown. Invert and align to make a rectangle. Blend by running through a pasta machine, making the rectangle the width of the machine. Fold sheet onto itself, run it through pasta machine to mix colors. Keep folding, mixing in same direction. Colors will begin blending. When finished, a graduated Skinner Blend is revealed. Make final sheet #3 thickness on pasta machine. Mist clay sheet with water to allow stamp to release from clay. Place stamp on clay, press stamp deep into clay. Slice across texture with polymer clay blade to even out surface. Work on a surface like acrylic or glass to keep clay from moving as you slice. Blade is sharp, slice thin sections at a time. This creates a ghost image because the mica has shifted during pressing. Do not slice too deeply or image will be lost. Run clay piece through pasta machine again to even the back side, run in same direction as before.

Adorned Tool

 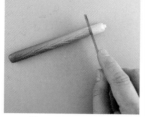  

Examples of
Skinner Blends.
See large detail below.

1 - 4 Prepare shaded clay strip, adhere to tool, joining seams exactly. Roll clay over a stamp, pressing firmly, texturing clay with stamp design. You may texture clay with an embossing tool. Find the seam, slice with slicer. You may have to recut after baking, this will be your guide. Decorate with slices of canes and sterling beads or bead cap. Bake on accordion folded cardstock to prevent flattening.

Adorned Brush

5 - 9 Roll with brayer to smooth surface. Coat wood tools with thin layer of White glue, allow to dry. Place clay strip on tool, press to tool. Trim clay strip. Add decorative pieces and faces. Bake as manufacturer directs.

Graduated Blend Leaf Cane for Adorned Brush

  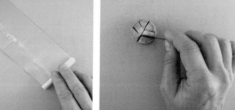 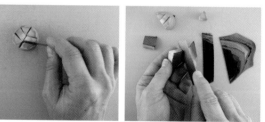

1 - 4 Make a sheet of Skinner Blended colors. Place sheet in pasta machine at light end of blend. Stretch sheet to thinnest setting. Sheet will be very long. Roll it up, starting with lightest color. Work it back into a larger diameter by pushing and rolling inward. Cut leaf into sections to suggest veins. Insert a very thin sheet of Brown between sections, reassemble leaf.

  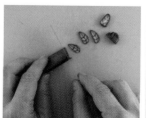 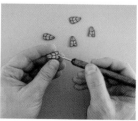

5 - 8 Wrap outside of leaf with a thin sheet of Brown. Press cane into a teardrop leaf shape. Pull cane to reduce and slice small leaves. Use small embossing tool to further shape leaf.

Skinner Blend Examples

Turn Plain Tools into Elegant Tools

Topped Tool
MATERIALS: *Excel* craft knife • Shaded sheet of clay (#3 Atlas) • Stamp with defined, deeply etched design from *Judikins* • *Sculpey* Super Slicer • Sterling bead cap • Variety of canes including face cane backed with white

Adorned Tool
MATERIALS: *Premo* pearl and metallic clays (mica shift clays) • Wood or metal tools or brushes to cover • Deeply etched rubber stamp from *Judikins* • *Crafter's Pick* Ultimate Tacky glue or Sobo White • Water and mist bottle • Acrylic Roller • Decorative Canes (see separate instructions)

Adorned Brush
Make Skinner Blend of clay following steps 1 - 3. Create decorative clay strips, steps 4 - 6. Attach strips to brush, steps 7-9. Embellish, step 10. Bake as the manufacturer directs.

by Barbara A. McGuire

Working with elegant tools inspires creative beginnings. In covering metal tools, clay will adhere to slick metal until it is cured permanently over and around the form.

When covering wood tools, first coat tool with a tacky surface. This can be Sobo, Crafter's Pick glue (allow to dry) or a thin layer of Liquid Sculpey. The tool can be decorated with ghost images, textures, embedded images and canes.

For a good finishing touch, put a sterling bead cap or wide bead at the top and where the tool joins the handle.

Transfer a poem or favorite saying onto clay to incorporate in an idea scroll. Use a face rubber stamp or a photo of a friend to create a wonderful gift. The poem is provided for you to copy to make this project.

The Idea
The idea seemed silly.
Absurd.
It was too complicated
        too dark
        too personal
Its shape was unfamiliar.
Its colors were murky
and wouldn't go with anything.
It got filed away
in the grey zone.
But
The idea was a pest
        gnawing
        fluttering
        biting
It drove me to distraction
and to my cluttered table
where the idea spilled out in a puddle
        and my paper
        scissors
        ink
        glue
        paint
        and brush
mopped it up.
There it was.
My idea.
Tangible and tactile
and pretty wonderful
        in an absurd way.

-Mary Lynn Maloney

The Idea Scroll
by Mary Lynn Maloney

MATERIALS: *Premo* clay (Purple, Black, Silver) • Super Slicer • Rubber stamps(*Printworks* Elegant Swirl #JB1855; *Limited Edition Face* #Jv128F) • Inks (*ColorBox* Eggplant; *Ancient Page* Sandalwood, Sage; *Memories* Black; *Marvy* Ochre, Bottle Green, Pale Violet; *Encore* Ultimate Metallic Teal) • Deco Art acrylic paint (Desert Turquoise, Dioxazine Purple) • *Craf-T Products* Metallic rub-ons • *Pearl Ex* powders (Red Russet, Interference Violet) • *Jacquard* Printable cotton fabric • Coffee and mister bottle • *E-6000* glue • *Gem-Tac* glue • *Xyron* 850 High tack • *Krylon* Matte Finish Spray • 5½" x 13¼" Matboard • 8½" x 17" Brown kraft paper • 5" x 5" Mulberry paper • Fiberfill • Hot glue • Steel Blue *Magic Leaf* • Palentino Linotype

INSTRUCTIONS: Condition clay. Roll out a 3" x 4" x ⅛" piece of Purple clay. Lay Elegant Swirl rubber stamp on work surface, rubber side up. Lay Purple clay diagonally over half of the stamp, lightly press clay into upturned rubber stamp. To roll scroll edges, set clay, impression side down, on work surface. Gently roll upper left edge of clay over on a diagonal, creating a cave-like shape on left side.

Condition, roll out Black clay into an irregularly shaped 4" x 9" rectangle as thin as possible. Using same rubber stamp, lay top short edge of clay onto rubber and impress image into clay. Repeat with bottom edge. Roll these edges inward to form top and bottom of scroll shape. Impress stamp along both long sides of scroll, forming a stamped border. Lay Purple clay piece at the top of Black scroll piece, gently push pieces together to join.

Roll a 1½" ball of Purple clay into an 8" snake. Center snake horizontally along upper roll of scroll, gently push into Black clay to join. Shape ends of the snake into coils. Repeat for bottom.

Typeset and print poem on fabric. Cut around poem. Mist with coffee to give stained look. Place a tuft of fiberfill in center of scroll, cover with poem, push edges of poem into Black clay.

Bake clay piece. When cool, rub Black scroll section with Turquoise and Purple acrylic paint. Highlight with Olive metallic rub-on. Rub Purple clay with Turquoise paint, then Russet and Interference Violet powders. Rub coils with Red Russet powder.

Work 1 teaspoon of Violet powder into Silver clay, roll into a flat sheet. Stamp with face using Black ink. Trim to fit into area of Purple clay. Bake face. When cool, rub edges with metallic rub-on. Dust face with Interference Violet powder. Position and attach with E-6000 adhesive.

Spray assembled pieces with matte spray. Drip hot glue around poem,. When cool, cover with Gold leaf. Remove excess with stiff brush. Crumple Brown kraft paper, smooth out. Rub Ochre, Bottle Green and Pale Violet ink pads over the paper surface. Spritz paper with water to run colors together. When paper is dry, run through *Xyron* machine to apply adhesive to back side. Lay paper adhesive side up, place matboard in center. Trim paper corners at a diagonal to reduce bulk, cover matboard by smoothing flaps around to back.

Spray covered matboard with matte spray. Using a generous amount of *Gem-tac* adhesive, glue clay piece to covered matboard. Let dry. Using metallic Teal ink randomly, stamp Elegant Swirl Tree onto mulberry paper. Tear paper on diagonal to create 2 triangles. Run paper through the *Xyron* machine, adhere to board at upper left and lower right corners. Smooth flaps to back.

Roll a 1" ball of the Silver clay with Interference Violet powder into an 8" snake. Shape into a double-edged spiral swirl. Make 2. Bake. When cool highlight with rub-ons and powders. Spray with matte spray. Glue swirls to corners with *Gem-Tac*.

The Idea
The idea seemed silly.
Absurd.
It was too complicated
        too dark
        too personal
Its shape was unfamiliar.
Its colors were murky
and wouldn't go with anything.
It got filed away
in the grey zone.
But
The idea was a pest
        gnawing
        fluttering
        biting
It drove me to distraction
and to my cluttered table
where the idea spilled out in a puddle
and my paper
        scissors
        ink
        glue
        paint
        and brush
mopped it up.
There it was.
My idea.
Tangible and tactile
and pretty wonderful
        in an absurd way.

        –Mary Lynn Maloney

Artistry

Complex Face Cane

1 - 2 Begin by mixing several clay opaque colors. Add tiny bits of Burnt Sienna, Red, Copper, Pink, Blue or White to Ecru to get a Flesh color you like. Divide the color into 3 parts. Lighten ⅓ portion with White, darken ⅓ portion with Sienna or Brown.

3 - 4 Use the same Red for lips as cheeks. Remain consistent within color palette. Use the same Brown throughout the face, to darken the flesh and for the brow. I rarely use straight Black except for pupils in eyes and the top eye line. Lower lip color should be slightly lighter than upper lip color. Colors for White of eyes, iris, brows, lips and outline clays are not translucent tints, they are opaque colors with bits of translucent for consistency. Once you have made this base range of colors, you can use it to tint the translucent clay. That will be the bulk of the face. Tint ¾ pound of translucent clay with mid range Flesh. Use only a 1" diameter ball to tint entire pound. Adjust, if color is too faint, add more Flesh. Mix remaining translucent with light and dark Flesh. Keep all colors in order so you won't get them confused. Size your picture to the exact size you will be making the cane. Shape translucent Flesh to the face in the picture.

5 - 6 Trace your picture, outlining features with pencil, trace again on back of tracing paper. Image is now facing correct way. Place drawing on translucent clay, rub with bone folder. This transfers graphite to clay and serves as a guide for building a cane. Set aside while you build the features of the face. Build features and size them according to drawing, cut out a corresponding section in face and replace cut area with built features.

Continued on page 45.

This technique shows how to build a face from your favorite picture or photo. Begin by mixing several opaque colors. The opaque colors will be mixed with translucent clay for the face.

Transfer the picture to the clay. This serves as a guide for building the face cane. Build the features and size them according to the drawing.

Next, cut out a corresponding section in the face and replace the cut out areas with the built cane features.

Although this technique is complex and lengthy, as you can see, the results are absolutely stunning.

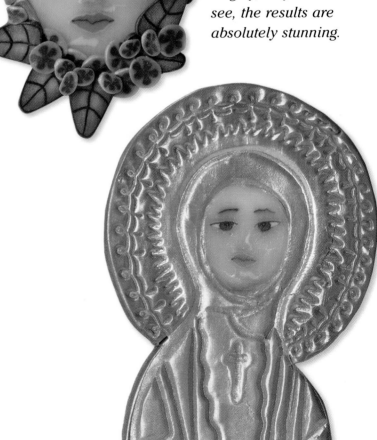

Complex Face Cane

Continued from page 45.

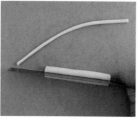

7 - 9 Starting with eyes, build a cane that can be cut in half making 2 eyes. Start with gleam in eye. This is a White dot that rests at the top of each eye. We will be making 1 big eye and stretching it into 2 eyes. If the dot ends up on one side, make sure it is on the same side in both eyes. You can get so detailed as to use a Skinner Blend (see page 40) to shade the iris of the eye. Roll blend into a cylinder with light-est color in the middle. Slice top 1/3 part of cylinder horizontally to insert the pupil. Make an indent with needle tool to accept pupil.

10 - 12 Place a snake of Black into indent for pupil. Slice to even top of the eye. Indent a ridge to accept the gleam of the eye. Throughout the entire process, we will indent or create the space for the next shape to fit into. Insert gleam in the eye.

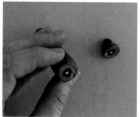

13 - 15 Place Black pupil and iris back on eye to rebuild center of the eye. Cut cane on both ends to see that it is accurate. If not, begin again. Begin to shape pieces for corners or whites of eyes. These are typically triangles with very subtle convex or concave curves. Look closely at your picture.

16 - 18 Place whites at corners of iris. Compare it to drawing, is the eye round? It is usually cut off at the top by the lid. Notice these small details throughout the process. Slice the top of the iris where the lid will fall. Wrap cylinder with the thinnest sheet possible of Black. Build shading around eyes. Wrap the entire unit in the lightest Flesh color, this will make eyes bright. I have wrapped 2 layers on top because the upper lid is wider.

It is astounding to look at a bead and realize what you are seeing is not paint nor a transferred picture, but a cane of assembled colors and shapes of clay. You will be making a huge face and reducing it. That is the trick to these tiny faces. The reality is that step by step, you can create a portrait in clay. It takes patience, careful observa-tion and a willingness to persevere to a final outcome. Your reward is a unique piece of artistry that lasts for years.

Before I begin to build the cane, my attention is completely on mixing the color. In most portrait canes I use translucent clay. Translucent clay blends together in shades instead of defined opaque sections. Mixing color is a personal decision. Color can also reflect ethnic identities. Color intensity or saturation can also make a differ-ence in the final results. I usually hold a thin portion of clay up to the light to look at the color before accepting what I have mixed.

Mix opaque colors in complete ranges, light, medium and dark, as well as color for eyes, cheeks and lips. It takes only a small amount of opaque clay to tint a whole pound of translu-cent clay. The final goal is to make a translucent cane that will be thinly sliced and backed by a layer of White. This is how to get a soft glowing look to the cane.

Artistry – Portrait in Clay

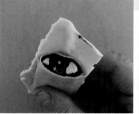    

19 - 23 Add another layer of medium Flesh on the top lid, creating the bulk of the eye lid. Place darkest Flesh on the top lid to create the lid line. Trim or smooth colors into each other to create subtle tapers to outlines. This helps make the lines more real. Wrap entire eye in Flesh. This wrapping is to encase eye so there is a continuous wrap creating a smooth outline. If pieces were added by section, sometimes small bits of clay leak in between sections. Wrap features consistently throughout cane. Your eye should be long enough to make 2 units of eye. Stretch eye if necessary to fit the proportion of the drawing.

24 - 27 Cut a piece from both ends of cane to make sure everything is in place. I usually save these pieces for reference. Compare eye to original drawing. The 2nd eye will be the cane turned around, smaller Whites will be on the inside of both eyes. Make 2 strips of Brown clay for eyebrows. Taper one end of strip by rolling brayer at an angle. Wrap brow in Flesh.

28 - 32 Now you are going to cut into the whole face to section it, remove and replace sections. Cut out square sections for eyes. Add triangle shapes of clay sliced from the area you cut out. Make a square section of eye to insert. Trim eye to fit exactly Make sure eyes are aligned correctly, front and back. Take forehead section, carve out the area for brow by bending the blade and carving down.

33 - 37 Smooth inside of holes before you insert brow. Place a crescent shape, sliced from removed brow, over eye and place brow on top of eye. Place a portion of Flesh between the eyes, replace forehead. Make lips by tapering both sides of a thick sheet of clay. Bottom lip is a lighter color than top. Make an indent in lower lip to allow for curve of the smile line. Top lip has 2 humps impressed in the sheet of darker lip clay.

    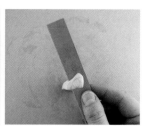

38 - 42 Place an extremely thin sheet of Brown clay between the lips to define the smile line. Trim any smile line clay before wrapping entire lip unit in dark Flesh. This Flesh was actually made a little darker just to outline the lips. Wrap entire unit in Flesh clay. Put a tiny triangle of Flesh clay between dents in upper lip to keep this area defined. Note: Any time you use clay from an extracted portion, remember to remove the graphite so it doesn't discolor the cane.

Continued on page 48.

Complex Face Cane

I hope you have as much fun trying face caning as I've had. Each portrait will bring new and challenging rewards. Remember, you can do it!

Continued from page 45.

  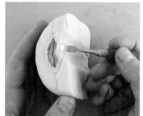

43 - 46 Wrap lips a second time. Slice on both ends to check design. Compare this with your face cane, stretch to proper proportion. Section face again, bend your blade to carve out a section for mouth. Smooth inside of carved section. Put lips in place.

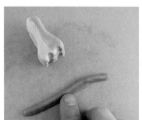    

47 - 51 Piece it together, pack firmly by packing it on all sides. Rotate and turn to distribute pressure throughout the cane. Once put together, cut it apart for the nose. The hole will help determine size of the nose. Make it a little smaller than you think, because in reduction, it is the nose that shrinks the least. A nose is not Black, but a combination of light and dark shades of Flesh. The nose shape is awkward to make. Make a triangle. This nose had ¾ Light Flesh and ¾ Dark Flesh, according to shadows in the original picture. Make dent for nostrils with brass tube.

52 - 56 Roll extra dark clay for the actual nostrils. After nostrils are in place, complete bulb of nose. Size the nose for insertion. Smooth out crevice for nose in the shape you are going to insert. Before nose is inserted, wrap the entire unit in Flesh.

62 - 66 Roll cheek cane to fit into both cheeks. If there are air bubbles, slice into the cane at an angle to release air and smooth the cane. Place cane, reassemble face. Pack the cane together as before. For the chin, cut a portion out by bending the blade. Chin needs a dark Flesh directly under mouth, a light Flesh on top of chin protrusion. Reassemble, trim outer layers of clay. They get dirty from handling and may not match. It is better to trim the clay than force it to displace any features.

Artistry - Portraits

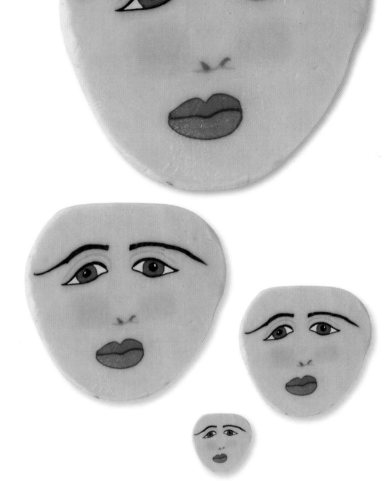

Start big then make your cane face any size you like.

57 - 61 Reassemble face, press together. Make cheeks with a slightly deepened or Pinker color of Flesh. Do not make cheeks too Rosy. Begin with a Skinner Blend of Flesh and cheek color. Make two. Roll into a shaded cylinder. The gradual blend makes the cheeks Rosy and contours the face. Punch out a cheek circle with a clean large brass tube just under eyes. Scrape inside of the hole to make sure it is smooth and clean.

67 - 69 Compare the cane to the drawing. Wrap it entirely with translucent clay. This adds extra to the outside which will probably stretch. Slice across top, see the face underneath.

Note: See Page 50 for Reduction instructions.

Now you are ready to make your own Expressive Faces in Clay

Reduction

1 - 2 For the reduction, add layers of translucent clay on top, bottom and each side. I added a darker shade of clay on sides. If the final face is proportionate, this serves as a slightly darker outline. Allow the clay to set for a while. This evens the temperature and aids consistent reduction. Add additional outside layers to prevent the outer layers from moving too fast, distorting the features. Package colors left from face in a heavy plastic bag to keep for neck and or ears.

3 - 4 To begin reduction, lift and bang cane on its side on a firm table. Rotate cane and change direction, so it gets even pressure on all sides.

5 - 6 When it is small enough to grab, squeeze from the middle, rotating and flipping it to get even pressure from all sides. When reduced to a workable size, you can pull it as well. Look inside to determine if adjustments should be made to bring the cane back into alignment.

7 - I like to save cane in large pieces as well as small pieces, because I can add different hair, neck, etc. to the beautiful cane I will have for many years.

Note: There is another way to stretch the cane once it is reduced to a workable size. Slice the ends to make an even, smooth surface and stick to glass or acrylic rounds. (If needed, use a little Liquid Sculpey to make it sticky.) Use the glass as handles to pull the cane apart. The suction pulls the middle as well as the outside of the cane.